THE LITTLE BOOK OF
PRIDE

First published in 2020 by OH!
An Imprint of Welbeck Non-Fiction Limited,
part of Welbeck Publishing Group.
Based in London and Sydney.
www.welbeckpublishing.com

ISBN 978-1-91161-046-5

Compiled and written by: Stella Caldwell
Editorial: Victoria Godden
Project manager: Russell Porter
Design: Tony Seddon
Production: Rachel Burgess

A CIP catalogue record for this book is available from the British Library

Printed in Dubai

10 9 8 7 6 5 4 3 2

THE LITTLE BOOK OF
PRIDE

LGBTQ+ VOICES
THAT CHANGED THE WORLD

CONTENTS

INTRODUCTION - 6

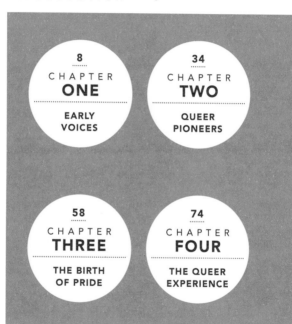

8

CHAPTER
ONE

EARLY
VOICES

34

CHAPTER
TWO

QUEER
PIONEERS

58

CHAPTER
THREE

THE BIRTH
OF PRIDE

74

CHAPTER
FOUR

THE QUEER
EXPERIENCE

104

CHAPTER
FIVE

OUT AND
PROUD!

132

CHAPTER
SIX

WISDOM

166

CHAPTER
SEVEN

THE FIGHT
GOES ON

INTRODUCTION

On a hot night in June 1969, a series of furious confrontations took place between the police and LGBTQ+ activists outside the Stonewall Inn in New York City. No one could have known it then, but the Stonewall riots would come to mark a historic moment in the push for LGBTQ+ rights, and the symbolic birth of an organized global movement.

The very first Pride march took place a year later, in June 1970. Named after the street where the Stonewall Inn was located, the Christopher Street Liberation Day march drew around 2,000 people. As leading activist Martha Shelley told a crowd: "The time has come for us to walk in the sunshine. We don't have to ask permission to do it. Here we are!"

There was a sense of hope as the new movement rapidly grew. At the time, it was incredibly difficult for LGBTQ+ people to publicly campaign. They feared social disapproval, losing their jobs or being arrested. But now there was a call to be unafraid: to end centuries of oppression and to find strength in numbers.

Of course, progress has not been universal and the struggle is far from over: homosexuality remains illegal in over 70 countries, and even in so-called tolerant societies, LGBTQ+ people can still face discrimination. However, 50 years on from that first Pride march, huge strides have been made for LGBTQ+ rights.

Today, hundreds of colourful Pride parades and parties take place around the world each year. This book is a celebration of the long journey to a place of pride. Beginning with the movement's earliest pioneers, it captures the voices of those who have dared to take a stand, of those who took the fight into the streets, and of those who continue to speak up for LGBTQ+ equality today.

CHAPTER
ONE

EARLY VOICES

My heart explodes within my breast;
One timid glance, and all my
   voice is gone,
My tongue breaks, and a
   subtle flame
Races below my flesh, my eyes
Refuse their sight, my hearing
   is a gong,
Cold sweat clings to me, and I shake
From head to toe...
I am about to die, I think...

Ancient Greek poet Sappho (the modern term "lesbian" comes from her home island of Lesbos), addressed to an unknown woman, Fragment 31, sixth century BC

“

Who would give a law to lovers?
Love is unto itself a higher law.
”

Boethius, The Consolation of Philosophy,
early sixth century

Shall I compare thee to a
    summer's day?
Thou art more lovely and more
temperate...

*William Shakespeare, many of whose
famous sonnets – including Sonnet
18 – were addressed to a mysterious
figure called the "Fair Youth", 1609*

"

I love, & only love, the fairer sex
& thus beloved by them in turn,
my heart revolts from any other
love than theirs.

"

Anne Lister, businesswoman,
world traveller and mountaineer,
writing in her diary, 1821

> **"**
> For the one I love most lay
>   sleeping by me under the same
>   cover in the cool night,
> In the stillness in the autumn
>   moonbeams his face was
>   inclined toward me,
> And his arm lay lightly around
>   my breast – and that night I
>   was happy.
> **"**

Walt Whitman, "When I Heard at the Close of the Day", Leaves of Grass, *1855*

> Until my dying day I will look back with pride that I found the courage to come face to face in battle against the spectre, which for time immemorial has been injecting poison into me and into men of my nature… Indeed, I am proud that I found the courage to deal the initial blow to the hydra of public contempt.

Karl Heinrich, "the father of gay rights", who in 1867 became the first person to publicly defend homosexuality, in Berlin

66

Love is as varied as people are.

99

Magnus Hirschfeld, who founded the first LGBTQ+ rights organisation, the Scientific-Humanitarian Committee, in Berlin in 1897

66

I am the love that dare not speak its name.

99

Lord Alfred Douglas, whose relationship with Oscar Wilde saw Wilde imprisoned, "Two Loves", 1892

Your sonnet is quite lovely, and it is a marvel that those red rose-leaf lips of yours should be made no less for the madness of music and song than for the madness of kissing. Your slim gilt soul walks between passion and poetry. I know Hyacinthus, whom Apollo loved so madly, was you in Greek days.

Letter from Oscar Wilde to Lord Alfred "Bosie" Douglas, June 1891

▼

"

To regret one's own experiences is to arrest one's own development. To deny one's own experiences is to put a lie into the lips of one's own life. It is no less than a denial of the soul.

"

Oscar Wilde, extract from "De Profundis", written in Reading Gaol after his conviction for gross indecency, 1897

Paris has always seemed to me the only city where you can live and express yourself as you please.

Openly lesbian poet, playwright and novelist Natalie Clifford Barney, writing in the early twentieth century

66

The most violent element in society is ignorance.

Emma Goldman, early twentieth-century activist and writer

99

I have you with me everywhere, see you and hear you and live with you. Once I can't do that anymore, I will long for you.

Selma Lagerlöf, Swedish author and the first woman to win the Nobel Prize for Literature, in 1909, in a letter to her companion Sophie Elkan

66

Look here Vita – throw over your man, and we'll go to Hampton Court and dine on the river together and walk in the garden in the moonlight and come home late and have a bottle of wine and get tipsy, and I'll tell you all the things I have in my head, millions, myriads… Think of that. Throw over your man, I say, and come.

99

Virginia Woolf, author of the ground-breaking novel Orlando, in a letter to Vita Sackville-West, 1927

Beside the strength and permanence and all enduring feeling which I have for you, everything else is shifting sand... My sweetheart, my beautiful, my lovely one.

Letter from influential anthropologist Margaret Mead to Ruth Benedict, with whom she had a passionate relationship for a quarter of a century until Benedict's death, 1928

Our love may be faithful even unto death and beyond – yet the world will call it unclean.

From the ground-breaking novel The Well of Loneliness (which was banned in Britain until 1959 for its frank portrayal of lesbianism), Radclyffe Hall, 1928

I am finished. Lili has known this for a long time. That's how matters stand. And consequently she rebels more vigorously every day.

Danish transgender pioneer Lili Elbe (subject of the 2015 film The Danish Girl)*, one of the first people to undergo gender reassignment surgery, writing in her journal, 1930*

"
Many highly respectable individuals of ancient and modern times have been homosexuals, several of the greatest men among them (Plato, Michelangelo, Leonardo da Vinci, etc). It is a great injustice to persecute homosexuality as a crime – and a cruelty, too.
"

The founder of psychoanalysis, Sigmund Freud, in a letter to a mother who asked him to treat her son's homosexuality, 1935

It is funny that men who are supposed to be scientific cannot get themselves to realise the basic principle of physics, that action and reaction are equal and opposite, that when you persecute people you always rouse them to be strong and stronger.

Author Gertrude Stein, who had an openly lesbian relationship with Alice B. Toklas in Paris, from 1907 until Stein's death in 1946

66

It is better to be hated for what you are than to be loved for what you are not.

99

André Gide, the first openly gay winner of the Nobel Prize for Literature in 1947

Only the human mind invents categories and tries to force facts into separated [pigeon-holes]. 🟊🟊

From Sexual Behaviour in the Human Male, *Alfred Kinsey's explosive book that rocked 1940s America by stating that 10 per cent of men are homosexual, 1948*

I'm not willing to just be tolerated. That wounds my love of love and of liberty.

Poet, playwright, novelist and filmmaker Jean Cocteau

We were up against a solid wall of ignorance, hypocrisy, meanness and corruption. The wall had won.

Henry Gerber, who in 1924 founded America's first gay rights organisation, the Society for Human Rights, writing in 1965

> **"**
> Wouldn't it be wonderful if all our letters could be published in the future in a more enlightened time. Then all the world could see how in love we are. **"**

Letter from Infantryman Gordon Bowsher to Gunner Gilbert Bradley during the Second World War, discovered in 2008

CHAPTER
TWO

QUEER
PIONEERS

Legislators have no right to veto nature; no right to persecute nature in the course of its work; no right to torture living creatures who are subject to those drives nature gave them.

Karl Heinrich Ulrichs, often considered the first gay activist, Research on the Riddle of "Man-Manly" Love, 1864–80

❝

Soon the day will come when
science will win victory over error,
justice a victory over injustice, and
human love a victory over human
hatred and ignorance. **❞**

*Magnus Hirschfeld, who founded the
first LGBTQ+ rights organisation,
the Scientific-Humanitarian Committee,
in Berlin in 1897*

Anyone who realises what Love is, the dedication of the heart, so profound, so absorbing, so mysterious, so imperative… cannot fail to see how difficult, how tragic even, must often be the fate of those whose deepest feelings are destined from the earliest days to be a riddle and a stumbling-block, unexplained to themselves, passed over in silence by others.

Poet, philosopher and early LGBTQ+ activist Edward Carpenter, The Intermediate Sex, *1908*

Different though the sexes are, they intermix. In every human being a vacillation from one sex to the other takes place, and often it is only the clothes that keep the male or female likeness, while underneath the sex is the very opposite of what it is above.

99

From Orlando, Virginia Woolf's ground-breaking novel exploring gender fluidity, 1928

66

I am, at heart, a gentleman.

99

Hollywood film star Marlene Dietrich

> **"**
> I am very proud now, looking back... It was the sexual revolution that was going to start with or without me. We may not have started it, but we gave it a good swift kick in the pants! **"**

Christine Jorgensen, a former GI in the US Army who underwent gender reassignment surgery in 1952 and became a celebrity

…not many people have ever died of love. But multitudes have perished, and are perishing every hour – and in the oddest places! – for the lack of it.

From Giovanni's Room, James Baldwin's pioneering novel about same-sex love, 1956

66

We hit it off, we started courting.
I flew to Boston [to see her] and
got off the plane with a big bunch
of flowers in my hand. I couldn't
resist. I did not care what the world
thought. I dropped the flowers,
grabbed her and kissed her. That
was not being done in 1961.

99

*Prominent activist Barbara Gittings, who
fought for LGBTQ+ rights for nearly five
decades, on her partner Kay Tobin Lahusen*

66

It was an absolute necessity for me to declare homosexuality, because if I didn't I was a part of the prejudice.

99

Civil rights activist Bayard Rustin, who masterminded the 1963 March on Washington but whose name was never widely known due to his sexuality

66

I know I'm perfectly as capable of being swayed by a girl as by a boy. More and more people feel that way and I don't see why I shouldn't.

99

Singer Dusty Springfield bravely comes out as bisexual in an interview, London Evening Standard, *1970*

I'm queer. But why would people get so upset about something that feels so good? Me being a queer can't hurt anyone, why should it be such a terrible thing? Makes no sense.

From ground-breaking lesbian novel Rubyfruit Jungle, *Rita Mae Brown, 1973*

I'm as gay as a daffodil, my dear!

Freddie Mercury responding to a question about his sexuality, New Musical Express, *1974*

It's true – I am a bisexual. But I can't deny that I've used that fact very well. I suppose it's the best thing that ever happened to me.

David Bowie, Playboy *magazine, September 1976*

"

If a bullet should enter my brain, let that bullet destroy every closet door.

"

Harvey Milk, one of the first openly gay people elected to public office, in a recording made shortly before his assassination in 1978

When I was in the military,
they gave me a medal for killing
two men and a discharge for
loving one.

*Tombstone of Vietnam War veteran Leonard
Matlovich, the first gay serviceman to publicly
out himself to fight the ban on LGBTQ+
people serving in the US military, 1988*

66

My struggle has allowed me to
transcend that sense of shame
and stigma identified with my
being a black gay man. Having
come through the fire, they can't
touch me.

99

Marlon Riggs, pioneering American
filmmaker who gave a voice to black
gay men in the 1980s and early 1990s

It is not our differences that divide us. It is our inability to recognise, accept and celebrate those differences.

Activist and writer Audre Lorde, who described herself as "black, lesbian, feminist, mother, poet warrior"

Yep, I'm Gay.

Ellen DeGeneres, comedian, actress and talk-show host, comes out to Time magazine shortly before her fictional sitcom counterpart, "Ellen", also came out in a first for primetime TV, 14 April 1997

Marriage is a magic word. And it is magic throughout the world. It has to do with our dignity as human beings, to be who we are openly.

LGBTQ+ rights activist Edie Windsor, who played a monumental role in the fight for marriage equality

I'm a 34-year old NBA centre.
I'm black. And I'm gay.

Basketball star Jason Collins becomes the
first current athlete in US professional sport
to come out, Sports Illustrated, 6 May 2013

It is revolutionary for any trans person to choose to be seen and visible in a world that tells us we should not exist.

Actress Laverne Cox, the first openly transgender person to be on the cover of Time magazine, Buzzfeed, 16 March 2014

"

It is absolutely imperative that every human being's freedom and human rights are respected, all over the world.

"

Jóhanna Sigurðardóttir, former prime minister of Iceland (2009–13) and the world's first openly gay head of government, World Pride, Toronto, 28 June 2014

CHAPTER
THREE

THE BIRTH
OF PRIDE

66

I'm not missing a moment of this – it's the revolution!

99

Transgender activist Sylvia Rivera at the Stonewall Riots, 1969

"

The queens got very vocal, and some of them started to pick things up and throw them at the police. At one point a police car came down Christopher Street, and five or six queens leapt on it and started jumping up and down on the roof, and the roof just caved in. More and more people arrived and started joining in.

"

Transgender singer Jayne County, who witnessed the Stonewall Riots in 1969

The protests went on for three days and the whole area around Christopher Street and Seventh Avenue was cordoned off… When someone shouted 'Gay is good' in imitation of 'Black is beautiful', we all laughed; at that moment we went from seeing ourselves as a mental illness to thinking we were a minority.

Edmund White, who witnessed the Stonewall Riots in 1969, The Guardian, *19 June 2019*

66

The time has come for us to walk in the sunshine. We don't have to ask permission to do it. Here we are!

99

Martha Shelley addressing a Gay Power vigil, New York, July 1969

The next time someone asks you why LGBT Pride marches exist or why Gay Pride Month is June, tell them 'A bisexual woman named Brenda Howard thought it should be.'

Brenda Howard, who was instrumental in organising America's first Pride marches in the 1970s

66

I will define myself to my government. I will not allow my government to define me…

99

LGBTQ+ activist Frank Kameny on why he took part in America's first Pride parade, Christopher Street Liberation Day, held in New York on 28 June 1970

Say it loud, gay is proud!

Official chant for New York's first Pride march, 28 June 1970

> We got mixed reactions from the public. Some were hostile. Many were curious or bewildered. Most had never knowingly seen a gay person, let alone hundreds of queers marching to demand freedom.

LGBTQ+ activist Peter Tatchell describing London's first Gay Pride march on 1 July 1972, HuffPost, 7 July 2017

Homosexuality is part of society,
I guess that they need more variety,
Freedom of expression is really
the thing.

From "Ain't Nobody Straight in LA"
by Motown group The Miracles, 1975

66

Burst down those closet doors once and for all, and stand up, and start to fight.

99

Harvey Milk, one of the first openly gay people to be elected to public office in the United States

Flags are torn from the soul of the people.

Gilbert Baker, creator of the Rainbow Flag

Equality means more than passing laws. The struggle is really won in the hearts and minds of the community, where it really counts.

Prominent LGBTQ+ activist
Barbara Gittings

"

On this anniversary of Stonewall,
I ask my gay sisters and brothers
to make the commitment to fight.
For themselves, for their freedom,
for their country… We will not win
our rights by staying quietly in
our closets…

"

*Speech by Harvey Milk, one of the first
openly gay people to be elected to public
office, San Francisco Pride parade, 1978*

We are powerful because
we have survived.

Audre Lorde, Sister Outsider:
Essays and Speeches, *1984*

CHAPTER
FOUR

THE QUEER
EXPERIENCE

What is straight? A line can be straight, or a street, but the human heart, oh, no, it's curved like a road through mountains.

Tennessee Williams, A Streetcar Named Desire, *1947*

66 Nature made a mistake, which I have corrected. **99**

Transgender pioneer Christine Jorgensen, who underwent gender reassignment surgery in 1952

66

Love him and let him love you.
Do you think anything else under
heaven really matters?

99

James Baldwin, Giovanni's Room, *1956*

66

In itself, homosexuality is as limiting as heterosexuality: the ideal should be to be capable of loving a woman or a man; either, a human being, without feeling fear, restraint or obligation.

99

*French writer and feminist
Simone de Beauvoir*

How many years has it taken people to realise that we are all brothers and sisters and human beings in the human race? I mean how many years does it take people to see that? We're all in this rat race together!

Transgender activist Marsha P. Johnson

66

I'm sorry, Mama. Not for what I am, but for how you must feel at this moment. I know what that feeling is, for I felt it for most of my life. Revulsion, shame, disbelief – rejection through fear of something I knew, even as a child, was as basic to my nature as the colour of my eyes.

99

Coming-out letter written by author Armistead Maupin to his mother, 1977

I want someone who is fierce and will love me until death and knows that love is as strong as death, and be on my side forever and ever.

From Oranges Are Not the Only Fruit, *Jeanette Winterson's coming-of-age novel about a lesbian girl, 1985*

▼

66

I like the word gay, though I think of myself more as queer. I believe the strength in my work comes from that perspective – my being an outsider.

99

Lesbian performance artist Holly Hughes

If you are in the closet and fall in love with someone of the same gender, it doesn't automatically remove the shame and fear that's kept you locked away. The love you are experiencing encourages you to face the reality that this is who you really are and also has the power to set you free.

From A Life of Unlearning: A Journey to Find the Truth, *Anthony Venn-Brown, 2007*

❝

If homosexuality is a disease, let's all call in queer to work: 'Hello. Can't work today, still queer.'

❞

*Stand-up comic and lesbian activist
Robin Tyler, Red Pepper, 10 July 2009*

I learned compassion from being discriminated against. Everything bad that's ever happened to me has taught me compassion.

Ellen DeGeneres, actress and comedian who faced a backlash after publicly coming out in 1997

"

We are all human beings in this world, so why not practise that love with one another? I think young people who can't come out or talk to their parents about who they are need to remember this: don't let all of those hiccups keep you from experiencing life and joy. I think whatever your thing is, it'll come naturally if you allow it to.

"

Activist for LGBTQ+ rights and HIV/AIDS awareness Cecelia Chung

I very much want to inject gay culture into the mainstream. It's not an underground tool for me. It's my whole life.

Lady Gaga, Out, September 2009

66

...there is a subtle difference between tolerance and acceptance... It's the chasm between being invited to a colleague's wedding with your same-sex partner and being able to slow-dance without the other guests whispering.

99

Jodi Picoult, award-winning author

I believe marriage isn't between a man and a woman but between love and love.

Lyrics from "We All Try" by singer Frank Ocean, 2011

> **"**
> Gender preference does not define you. Your spirit defines you. **"**

From Awakened, P.C. *Cast, 2011*

As of today, patriotic Americans in uniform will no longer have to lie about who they are in order to serve the country they love.

Former president Barack Obama announces an end to the military ban on open homosexuality in the US military, 20 September 2011

> **❝**
> It takes some intelligence and insight to figure out you're gay and then a tremendous amount of balls to live it and live it proudly. **❞**

Jason Bateman, actor and LGBTQ+ activist

"

Putin needed an enemy,
an Other, against which to
mobilise. LGBT people are really
convenient: we're sort of the
ultimate foreign agent.

"

*Russian-American journalist
Masha Gessen, 3 February 2014*

66

Every LGBTQ+ refugee has a unique situation – but the fear and pain they endured before coming to Canada is universal.

99

Iranian refugee and LGBTQ+ rights activist Arsham Parsi

Amazing how eye and skin colour come in many shades yet many think sexuality is just gay or straight.

Dr DaShanne Stokes, who came out as bisexual in 2016

66

I've been embraced by a new
community. That's what happens
when you're finally honest about
who you are; you find others
like you.

99

Transgender activist Chaz Bono

Being LGBT is not a choice. It's not about 'a sexual proclivity'. It's not a 'lifestyle'… It's about our identity. Pride is a time when we come together to celebrate our community and when others do, too. Just as we do for other racial, ethnic, and religious groups that are part of the 'tossed salad' nature of our society.

Journalist Steven Petrow,
Washington Post, *21 June 2016*

> **"**
> The true ugliness of the closet is its subtlety. It eats away at your soul bit by bit and you don't even realize it. If you never deal with it or come to terms with it, then ultimately the closet will destroy you. **"**

From Sin Against the Race,
Gar McVey-Russell, 2017

66

I don't think homosexuality is a choice. Society forces you to think it's a choice, but in fact, it's in one's nature. The choice is whether one expresses one's nature truthfully or spends the rest of one's life lying about it.

99

Feminist actress, author and activist
Marlo Thomas

" A huge part of what animates homophobia among young people is paranoia and fear of their own capacity to be gay themselves. **"**

Dan Savage, author, journalist and LGBTQ+ activist

I've been attracted mostly to 'shes' but I've been with many people and I'm open to love whatever it can be.

Actor Ezra Miller

Normal, you see, is whatever you want it to be.

Cara Delevingne, Mirror Mirror, *2017*

CHAPTER
FIVE

OUT AND PROUD!

66

You're looking at a
roaring dyke!

*Broadcaster Jackie Forster
comes out at a 1969 rally*

> **"** Personally, coming out was one of the most important things I've ever done, lifting from my shoulders the millstone of lies that I hadn't even realised I was carrying. **"**

Sir Ian McKellen, who came out in response to the notorious British law introduced in 1988 called Section 28

I just wish more of my fellow queers would come out sometimes. It's nice out here, you know?

Singer Elton John accepting a Distinguished Achievement Award at the Los Angeles Gay and Lesbian Center, 23 November 1996

If Harry Potter taught us anything it's that no one should live in a closet.

J. K. Rowling announces that wizard Albus Dumbledore is gay, Carnegie Hall, New York, 19 October 2007

I don't think it should be a
surprise for anyone to hear
that I'm gay.

Singer Adam Lambert, 2009

"

I hope that somewhere in Small Town, USA, a fifteen-year-old kid looks to me as a role model the way I looked at the Indigo Girls and Elton John as role models.

"

Singer-songwriter Brandi Carlile on coming out as a lesbian, 2009

I am proud to say that I am a fortunate homosexual man. I am very blessed to be who I am. These years in silence and reflection made me stronger and reminded me that acceptance has to come from within, and that this kind of truth gives me the power to conquer emotions I didn't even know existed.

Singer and actor Ricky Martin comes out on his website, 29 March 2010

Having to hide something like that just ruined me. It really, really killed me.

Actress Portia de Rossi speaking to Oprah Winfrey about her struggles before coming out in 2005, November 2010

I have lived my life very openly and have never hidden the fact that I am gay. Apparently the prerequisite to being a gay public figure is to appear on the cover of a magazine with the caption 'I am gay'. I apologise for not doing so if this is what was expected!

Singer Jonathan Knight comes out on The New Kids on the Block blog, January 2011

66

My family knew I was gay when I was fifteen… But it's a very different thing coming out to your family and coming out to the universe. That's a big step. Maybe without me, there wouldn't be Adam Lambert. Without Bowie, there wouldn't be me. Without Quentin Crisp, there wouldn't have been Bowie. So everything is part of a big daisy chain.

99

Singer Boy George, Hollywood Reporter, *23 February 2011*

This is how I was born. I mean, there's no doubt in my mind.

Chaz Bono speaking after his gender reassignment surgery, ABC News, 9 May 2011

"

It's so liberating… This is my coming out ball. I've been dying to do this.

"

Actor Sean Maher comes out,
September 2011

The most important thing is to
be honest about yourself. Secrets
weigh heavy and it's when you try
to keep everything to yourself that
it becomes a burden. You waste
energy agonising when you could
be living your life and realising
your dreams.

*Nicola Adams, two-times Olympic
gold medallist and world champion boxer,
on her bisexuality*

❝

The fact is, I'm gay, always have been, always will be, and I couldn't be any more happy, comfortable with myself, and proud.

❞

Journalist Anderson Cooper in a public email to Andrew Sullivan on The Daily Beast, *2 July 2012*

It's been a journey and a process of becoming totally out and sort of living that truth and having it be a daily thing. I'm at the point now that I want people to know that, and I want to talk about it. We're coming so far as a society, but we still have so far to go. So, until we're all the way there, I'll probably die talking about it.

Megan Rapinoe, professional football player, 2012

> **"**
> I am a strong, black, lesbian
> woman. Every single time I say it,
> I feel so much better. **"**

Brittney Griner, basketball star, 2013

It felt like it was my dirty little secret… it felt like I had chains wrapped around me. I couldn't say anything; I couldn't be who I wanted to be. I felt so alone and trapped in who I was.

Olympic swimmer Tom Daley speaking on The Jonathan Ross Show *about his decision to come out, December 2013*

"

I am tired of hiding and I am tired of lying by omission. I suffered for years because I was scared to be out… I'm standing here today, with all of you, on the other side of that pain.

"

Actress Ellen Page comes out, Human Rights Campaign's Time to Thrive conference, Las Vegas, 14 February 2014

To anyone out there especially young people feeling like they don't fit in and will never be accepted, please know this, great things can happen when you have the courage to be yourself.

Footballer star Michael Sam, who came out in 2014

66

I am a gay man, it's not a secret, but not something that everyone would necessarily know… It's just part of who I am, it doesn't define me, it is part of my character I suppose.

99

Irish prime minister Leo Varadkar in an interview with RTÉ's Miriam O'Callaghan, January 2015

I read an article a few months ago by Sir Ian McKellen and he said no openly gay man had won an Oscar. If this is the case, I want to dedicate this to the LGBT community around the world. I stand here tonight as a proud gay man and I hope that we can all stand as equals one day.

Singer Sam Smith receives an Oscar for best original song, 29 February 2016

66

It's just who I am. I have absolutely no issue with it whatsoever, and I don't really care if other people have an issue with it.

99

Actress Gillian Anderson discusses her bisexuality, Daily Mail, 3 February 2018

I've never been interested in being invisible and erased.

Actress and LGBTQ+ advocate Laverne Cox, the first openly transgender person to be nominated for a Primetime Emmy Award and the first to feature on the cover of Time magazine

"

I can't spend my life worrying about others. No one can live without love.

"

Dutee Chand, athlete and LGBTQ+ activist in India, The Guardian, *10 June 2019*

It made my art more real, raw, honest, less manufactured and less fake.

Singer-songwriter Andrea di Giovanni on how embracing his queerness helped his art, 2019

"

I can't believe I'm saying this today, to all of you, for the entire world to see, but damn, it feels good to finally do it. It's time to let go and be truly free. When I was younger I was born in the wrong body, which means that I am transgender.

"

Beauty blogger Nikkie de Jager, known as NikkieTutorials, comes out, 13 January 2020

CHAPTER
SIX

WISDOM

All human beings are born free and equal in dignity and rights. They are endowed with reason and conscience and should act towards one another in a spirit of brotherhood.

Article I of the Universal Declaration of Human Rights, 10 December 1948

"

...only one thing is more frightening than speaking your truth. And that is not speaking.

"

Writer, feminist and activist Audre Lorde

66

Hell hath no fury like a drag queen scorned.

99

Sylvia Rivera, a transgender rights activist who was at the Stonewall Riots in 1969

❝

I think gay people are like blondes: there are fewer of them but they have more fun.

❞

Author and activist Rita Mae Brown

Everybody's journey is individual. You don't know with whom you're going to fall in love… If you fall in love with a boy, you fall in love with a boy. The fact that many Americans consider it a disease says more about them than it does about homosexuality.

Author James Baldwin, interview with
Eve Auchincloss and Nancy Lynch, 1969

66

You don't have to live a lie. Living a lie will mess you up. It will send you into depression. It will warp your values.

99

Gilbert Baker, creator of the Rainbow Flag

All young people, regardless of sexual orientation or identity, deserve a safe and supportive environment in which to achieve their full potential.

Harvey Milk, one of the first openly gay people elected to public office, 1977

"

The only queer people are those who don't love anybody.

"

Author and activist Rita Mae Brown,
28 August 1982

Please remember, especially in these times of group-think and the right-on chorus, that no person is your friend (or kin) who demands your silence, or denies your right to grow and be perceived as fully blossomed as you were intended.

From In Search of Our Mothers' Gardens: Womanist Prose, *Alice Walker, 1983*

66

You always have to remember
– no matter what you're told
– that God loves all the flowers,
even the wild ones that grow on
the side of the highway.

99

LGBTQ+ rights activist and singer
Cyndi Lauper

From the time I was a kid, I have never been able to understand attacks upon the gay community. There are so many qualities that make up a human being... By the time I get through with all the things that I really admire about people, what they do with their private parts is probably so low on the list that it is irrelevant.

Paul Newman, actor, director and vocal supporter of LGBTQ+ rights

❝

I am who I am because of the people who influenced me growing up, and many of them were gay. No one has any right to tell anyone what makes a family.

❞

*American actress and director
Drew Barrymore*

Find out who you are and be that person. That's what your soul was put on this Earth to be. Find that truth, live that truth, and everything else will come.

Ellen DeGeneres, comedian, actress and talk-show host

"

Hatred is not nature. It is nurture. No one is born with hatred in their heart – it is learned behaviour. People learn to hate in the same way they learn to love. The difference is: who are the educators?

"

Judy Shepard, mother of Matthew Shepard who was murdered in a hate crime in 1998

I've always felt that homophobic attitudes and policies were unjust and unworthy of a free society and must be opposed by all Americans who believe in democracy. The civil rights movement thrives on unity and inclusion, not division and exclusion. My husband's struggle parallels that of the gay rights movement.

Coretta Scott King, wife of Martin Luther King Jr, Chicago Sun Times, *1 April 1998*

66

Why is it that, as a culture,
we are more comfortable
seeing two men holding guns
than holding hands?

99

Author Ernest J. Gaines

Labels are for filing. Labels are for clothing. Labels are not for people.

Tennis legend Martina Navratilova

66

I believe that telling our stories, first to ourselves and then to one another and the world, is a revolutionary act.

99

Transgender rights activist, author and TV host Janet Mock

Never be bullied into silence.
Never allow yourself to be made a
victim. Accept no one's definition
of your life; define yourself.

Actor and playwright Harvey Fierstein

❝

You don't have to be gay to
be a supporter – you just have
to be a human.

❞

Daniel Radcliffe, 2010

We should indeed keep calm in the face of difference, and live our lives in a state of inclusion and wonder at the diversity of humanity.

George Takei, from Lions and Tigers and Bears: The Internet Strikes Back, *2013*

"

We are made for goodness.
We are made for love... We are
made to tell the world that there
are no outsiders. All are welcome:
black, white, red, yellow, rich,
poor, educated, not educated,
male, female, gay, straight,
all, all, all.

"

Archbishop Desmond Tutu,
Nobel Peace Prize winner

66

The pressures on gay teens can be overwhelming – to keep secrets, tell lies, deny who you are, and try to be who you're not. Remember: you are special and worth being cared about, loved, and accepted just as you are. Never, ever let anyone convince you otherwise.

99

Alex Sánchez, author of teen novels

Race, gender, religion, sexuality, we are all people and that's it. We're all people. We're all equal.

YouTuber Connor Franta, whose coming-out video in 2014 went viral

“

Love is never wrong.

”

Singer-songwriter and LGBTQ+ activist Melissa Etheridge

"
There's nothing wrong with you. There's a lot wrong with the world you live in. **"**

Actor Chris Colfer

We ask ourselves, who am I to be brilliant, gorgeous, talented, fabulous? Actually, who are you not to be?

Politician, author and activist Marianne Williamson

"

If I was to go back, I'd like to go and have a wee word with myself and say, 'You can fall in love with who you want to. You can be exactly who you want to be, you can run towards yourself if you like, because it's going to be fine.' **"**

Jackie Kay, Scottish Poet Laureate,
Elle, 2 May 2017

66

Love has no gender – compassion has no religion – character has no race.

99

From Either Civilized or Phobic: A Treatise on Homosexuality, *Abhijit Naskar, 2017*

"

Never apologise for being you.

Actor and singer John Barrowman, message to London Pride, 2018

"

Laverne Cox's struggle may look different than mine, but the pain we feel is the same… Someone who may be asexual may have a different journey than mine, but… there's things that we have in common… We have to support each other… we have to educate each other about our own individual journeys, because at the end of the day, we're all we got.

Actress, producer and screenplay writer Lena Waithe, GLAAD awards, 12 April 2018

66

Only you know who you were born to be, and you need to be free to be that person.

99

Model and actress Ruby Rose, who identifies as gender fluid

CHAPTER
SEVEN

THE FIGHT
GOES ON

Someday, the AIDS crisis will be over… And when that day comes… there'll be people alive on this earth – gay people and straight people, men and women, black and white – who will hear the story that once there was a terrible disease… and that a brave group of people stood up and fought… so that other people might live and be free.

AIDS activist Vito Russo addressing a crowd at an ACT UP demonstration two years before his death from an AIDS-related illness, Washington DC, 10 October 1988

ACT UP has taught everyone that you don't get anything by being nice, good little boys and girls. You do not get more with honey rather than vinegar.

AIDS activist and co-founder of ACT UP Larry Kramer, 1989

Silence=Death / Action=Life

The slogan used by ACT UP to draw attention to the HIV/AIDS crisis in the United States

> **We're here. We're queer. Get used to it!**

The slogan popularised by LGBTQ+ rights group Queer Nation in the 1990s

We will not go away with our issues of sexuality. We are coming home. It is not enough to tell us that one was a brilliant poet, scientist, educator, or rebel. Whom did he love? It makes a difference. "

Essex Hemphill, Ceremonies: Prose and Poetry, *1992*

▼

> **"**
> You don't have to be straight to be
> in the military; you just have to be
> able to shoot straight. **"**

*American politician Barry Goldwater
criticises the ban on open homosexuality
in the military, 11 June 1993*

Understand that sexuality is as wide as the sea. Understand that your morality is not law. Understand that we are you. Understand that if we decide to have sex whether safe, safer, or unsafe, it is our decision and you have no rights in our lovemaking.

Film director and LGBTQ+ rights activist Derek Jarman, who was open about his personal struggle with AIDS before his death

> **"** Gender is the poetry each of us makes out of the language we are taught. **"**

From Trans Liberation: Beyond Pink or Blue, *Leslie Feinberg, 1999*

There will not be a magic day when we wake up and it's now OK to express ourselves publicly. We make that day by doing things publicly until it's simply the way things are.

Speech by first openly gay senator Tammy Baldwin at the Millennium March for Equality, Washington DC, 30 April 2000

66

All people deserve to be treated
with dignity and have their human
rights respected, no matter who
they are or whom they love.
99

*Hillary Clinton, former US Secretary of
State, Human Rights Day speech,
Geneva, 6 December 2011*

I think it is important for someone like me to not run away from who I am but embrace it. LGBT people across the country need to know they have a friend in Congress.

Mark Takano, the first openly gay person of Asian descent in Congress, 29 April 2013

66

Openness may not completely disarm prejudice, but it's a good place to start. **99**

Basketball player Jason Collins,
Sports Illustrated, 6 May 2013

I don't want you to love me. I don't want you to like me. But I don't want you to beat me up and kill me. You don't have to like me, I don't care. But please don't kill me.

Kristen Beck, the first openly transgender former US Navy SEAL, in an interview with Anderson Cooper, 6 June 2013

▼

> This world would be a whole lot better if we just made an effort to be less horrible to one another. If we took just five minutes to recognise each other's beauty, instead of attacking each other for our differences.

Actress Ellen Page at the Human Rights Campaign's Time to Thrive conference, Las Vegas, 14 February 2014

We are all assigned a gender at birth. Sometimes that assignment doesn't match our inner truth... I was not born a boy, I was assigned boy at birth. Understanding the difference between the two is crucial to our culture and society moving forward in in the way we treat – and talk about – transgender individuals...

Supermodel Geena Rocero comes out as transgender while giving a TED talk in New York City, March 2014

▼

66

When all Americans are treated as equal, no matter who they are or whom they love, we are all more free.

99

Barack Obama, Twitter, 8 May 2014

I believe that love comes in all different shapes, sizes and colours. So whether you're LGBT or straight, your love is valid, beautiful, and an incredible gift.

Singer and actress Demi Lovato, face of the Human Rights Campaign's "Americans for Marriage Equality" movement, 2014

We declare that human rights are
for all of us, all the time: whoever
we are and wherever we are from;
no matter our class, our opinions,
our sexual orientation.
99

*Ban Ki-moon, former UN Secretary-General,
New York, 10 December 2014*

Coming out as gay was an easy enough matter for me, since I worked in a profession where being gay had a long history of being accepted… The number of letters I got in those early days from teenagers and from their parents thanking me for making them feel less alone gave me enormous heart and convinced me that I was on the right road.

Actor, comedian and writer Stephen Fry,
Out Front, *10 November 2014*

❝

I appeal to all governments and societies to promote the values of tolerance and respect for diversity, and to build a world where no one has to be afraid because of their sexual orientation and gender identity.

❞

António Guterres, Secretary-General of the United Nations, May 2015

If I wait for someone else to validate my existence, it will mean that I'm short-changing myself.

LGBTQ+ visual activist and photographer Zanele Muholi

"

Equality never comes easy… It was true of women fighting for suffrage… it was true of Australia's first peoples, who have fought to be truly recognised as citizens of our nation; and it has been true for lesbian, gay, bisexual, transgender and intersex Australians fighting for equality before the law.

"

Penny Wong, Australia's first openly gay senator, after Australia decisively voted t o support same-sex marriage, 14 November 2017

Every single day, people face
violence, jail time, death threats,
or worse, just because of who they
are or who they love.

Matt Beard, Executive Director at All Out,
July 2018

"

Fighting for all marginalised people is a duty and an honour I could not turn my back on nor will I ever.

"

Longtime LGBTQ+ champion
Madonna receives the Advocate for Change
Award at the GLAAD Media Awards,
4 May 2019

My activism does not need proof to be real. It exists in the work of my bones against weight in the morning.

Amandla Stenberg, actress and LGBTQ+ activist who identifies as non-binary